REALME GT 6T USER GUIDE

A Quick And Simple Beginner Reference Manual To Mastering The Features Of Your New Smartphone

By

Clinton J. Maxwell

© **2024 by Clinton J. Maxwell**

All rights reserved. No part of this book may be reproduced or used in any manner without the express written permission of the publisher except for the use of brief quotations in a book review.

DISCLAIMER

While every effort has been made to ensure the accuracy of the information in this book, the author and publisher do not assume and hereby disclaim any liability to any party for any loss, damage, or disruption caused by errors or omissions, whether such errors or omissions result from negligence, accident, or any other cause.

Table Of Contents

Introduction   7
   Getting Acquainted With Your New Tech Companion   7

Chapter 1: Parts of the REALME GT 6T   11
   Understanding The Device Layout And Buttons   11
   Exploring The Phone's Design And Features   12

Chapter 2: Setting Up Your REALME GT 6T   19
   Inserting The SIM And SD Card   19
   Powering On and Charging Up   20
   Setting Up Your Language And Region   21

Chapter 3: Camera Quality and Features   23
   Understanding The Camera Settings And Modes   23
   Using The Triple Camera Setup   26
   Tips for Taking Stunning Photos   27

Chapter 4: Advanced Camera Features   30
   Using Portrait Mode And Bokeh Effects   30
   Night Mode And Low Light Photography   32

Chapter 5: Navigation and Gestures   34
   Using The Home Screen And Navigation Bar   34

Chapter 6: Basic Phone Operations   38
   Making And Receiving Calls   38
   Sending And Receiving Texts And MMS   39
   Using The Phone Book And Contacts   41

Chapter 7: Understanding Settings	43
Exploring The Settings App	43
Customising Your Phone's Settings	44
Chapter 8: Screenshot and Screen Recording	47
How To Take Screenshots	47
How To Do Screen Recording	49
Chapter 9: How to Download and Install Apps	52
Using The Google Play Store	52
Installing Apps From Unknown Sources	54
Chapter 10: Managing Your Apps	57
How To Organise Your Apps	57
How To Uninstall And Update Apps	58
Chapter 11: How to Transfer Data from Your Old Phone	60
Using The REALME GT 6T's Builtin Transfer Tool	60
Transferring Data Using A Computer	62
Chapter 12: How to Use the REALME GT 6T's Advanced Features	66
How To Use The Phone's AI Features	66
How To Customise Your Phone's Theme And Wallpaper	68
Chapter 13: How to Set Up and Use Your Google Account	71
New to the Googleverse? How To Create Your Account	71
How To Sync Your Data And Contacts	74
Chapter 14: How to Use the Camera And Take	

Stunning Videos	77
Understanding Video Modes And Settings	77
How To Use The Triple Camera Setup	80
Chapter 15: How to Customise Your Home Screen and Notifications	83
How To Add And Remove Widgets	83
How To Customise Your Notification Shade	85
Chapter 16: How to Troubleshoot Common Issues	88
How To Fix Common Problems And Errors	88
How To Use The Builtin Troubleshooting Tools	91
Chapter 17: How to Update and Back Up Your Phone	94
How To Update Your Phone's Software	94
How To Back Up Your Data And Contacts	96
Conclusion	100
Summary Of Key Takeaways	100
Tips For Getting The Most Out Of Your REALME GT 6T	102

Introduction

Welcome to the REALME GT 6T User Guide! This comprehensive guide is your one-stop shop for mastering every feature your new smartphone has to offer. Whether you're a seasoned smartphone user or a complete newbie, this guide will walk you through everything you need to know, from setting up your phone to exploring its hidden gems.

Getting Acquainted With Your New Tech Companion

Unboxing Your Realme GT 6T: A Treasure Trove of Tech

Cracking open the box of your brand new Realme GT 6T is like stepping into a world of potential. Here's what you'll find inside:

- *The Realme GT 6T Smartphone*: The star of the show! This sleek and powerful device is ready to become an extension of you.
- *USB Type-C Cable*: This trusty cable is your lifeline for charging your phone and connecting it to your computer.

- *Power Adapter*: Never run out of juice! This adapter will keep your phone powered up and ready to go.
- *SIM Ejector Tool*: A tiny but mighty tool that helps you pop in your SIM card and get connected.
- *Quick Start Guide*: A handy booklet with a quick overview of getting started.
- *Safety Information*: Important information to ensure the safe and proper use of your phone.

Powering Up and Setting Sail: Your Initial Setup

Now that you've admired your new phone, let's get it up and running!

1. *Find the Power Button*: It's usually on the right side of the phone. Press and hold it for a few seconds until the Realme logo lights up the screen.
2. *Choose Your Language*: Let your phone know your preferred language so it can speak your tongue!
3. *Connect to Wi-Fi*: Find your Wi-Fi network, enter the password, and voila! You're connected to the world wide web.
4. *Sign in to Your Google Account*: This unlocks a universe of apps, services, and personalised

settings. Don't have a Google account? No worries, you can create one during this process.

5. *Setting Up Your Preferences*: This is where you can personalise your phone to your liking. Choose your date & time format, set up a screen lock (like a PIN or fingerprint) to keep your data secure, and explore other customization options.

Exploring the Realme UI: Your User-Friendly Command Center

The Realme GT 6T runs on the Realme UI, a user interface known for being intuitive and easy to navigate. Let's get familiar with the key areas:

- *Home Screen*: This is your landing pad after unlocking your phone. Here, you'll find your favourite apps, widgets (mini apps that provide quick information or functionality), and shortcuts all neatly organised.
- *Notification Panel*: Swipe down from the top of the screen to see all your notifications and access quick settings like Wi-Fi, Bluetooth, and brightness control. Think of it as your phone's central nervous system.
- *App Drawer*: Swipe up from the bottom of your home screen to see a list of all the apps installed on your phone. No more hunting for that specific game or social media app!

❖ *Settings*: This is where the magic happens. Represented by a gear icon, the Settings menu lets you personalise almost every aspect of your phone, from ringtones to battery optimization.

This is just the beginning of your Realme GT 6T adventure! We'll delve deeper into each feature, explore hidden functionalities, and equip you with tips and tricks to make the most of your powerful new smartphone companion.

Chapter 1: Parts of the REALME GT 6T

Welcome to the world of the REALME GT 6T! This powerhouse is designed to be an extension of you, seamlessly fitting into your life and amplifying your mobile experience. Let's embark on a journey to familiarise yourself with its layout, design, and the amazing features it offers.

Understanding The Device Layout And Buttons

Pick up your GT 6T and admire the phone's sleek design. The front is dominated by a stunning, expansive display. Imagine yourself watching videos or gaming on this beauty – the visuals will be nothing short of breathtaking. Nestled discreetly at the top middle sits a tiny punch-hole housing the front camera, perfect for capturing those selfies and video calls. Flip the phone over, and you'll be greeted by the innovative camera module. This isn't just a bump on the back; it's a powerhouse waiting to unleash your inner photographer. The main camera promises crystal-clear captures, while the ultra-wide lens lets you fit the whole world (or at least your entire group of friends) into one shot. The realme logo sits proudly below, a subtle reminder of the cutting-edge technology you now hold.

Exploring The Phone's Design And Features

Now, let's navigate the phone's controls. On the right side, your thumb naturally finds the power button, you'll also find the volume buttons – perfect for adjusting the sound to your liking during that nail-biting game or jamming out to your favourite tunes. The bottom side also houses the SIM card tray, the gateway to connecting you to the world, it also has an in-display fingerprint, a gentle touch unlocks your phone in a flash, keeping your data secure and private.

Take a peek at the top and bottom of the phone. The top is clean and minimalistic, with just a secondary microphone for superior noise cancellation during calls. Flip it over, and you'll find the all-important USB Type-C port for charging and data transfer. Nestled beside it are the primary microphone for clear voice capture, the speaker grille for booming audio, and to the delight of many.

Beyond the Basics: Unveiling the GT 6T's Features

The GT 6T boasts more than just a beautiful design; it's packed with features designed to elevate your smartphone experience. Let's delve deeper:

* *A Visual Feast*: The AMOLED Display – Get ready to be mesmerised by the large AMOLED display. Colours come alive with stunning vibrancy, while deep blacks create incredible contrast for an immersive viewing experience. Whether you're browsing photos, watching movies, or gaming, the visuals will leave you wanting more.

* *Powerhouse Performance*: – The GT 6T is equipped with a high-performance processor, the engine that makes everything tick. This powerhouse ensures smooth and responsive performance, no matter what you throw at it. Multitasking, running

demanding apps, or playing graphics-intensive games – the GT 6T handles it all with ease.

* *Fueling Your Day*: The Long-Lasting Battery – Who wants to be caught with a dead phone? The GT 6T boasts a large battery capacity, ensuring you can stay connected, entertained, and productive throughout the day. Stream videos, play games, chat with friends – the GT 6T won't let you down. When it's finally time to recharge, the incredibly fast charging technology will get you back up and running in no time.

* *Capture Memories Like a Pro*: The Camera System – The GT 6T's camera system is more than just a way to capture moments; it's your gateway to creative expression. The main camera captures stunningly detailed photos, while the ultra-wide lens lets you capture expansive landscapes or group photos without anyone getting left out. Feeling artistic? Explore features like night mode for stunning low-light shots and portrait mode for beautiful bokeh effects.

* *Your Personalised Experience*: The REALME UI – The GT 6T runs on REALME UI, a user-friendly interface based on the Android operating system. This software offers a range of features and

customization options, allowing you to tailor your phone to perfectly suit your needs and preferences. From themes and wallpapers to shortcuts and gestures, create a phone that feels as unique as you are.

Mastering Your Mobile Companion
Remember, the true beauty of the GT 6T lies in its potential for exploration. Don't be afraid to dive into the settings, experiment with different features, and personalise your phone to make it truly yours. The more you explore, the more you'll discover the incredible capabilities

Taking Photos and Videos Like a Pro
Let's delve a bit deeper into that impressive camera system. The main camera boasts a high megapixel count, which translates to capturing crisp and detailed photos that you can proudly share or print. The wide aperture allows more light to enter the sensor, resulting in excellent low-light performance. Say goodbye to blurry or grainy photos in those dimly lit environments!

But the GT 6T isn't a one-trick pony. The ultra-wide camera is perfect for capturing those breathtaking vistas or cramming your entire squad into a group photo without anyone missing the shot. Imagine capturing the grandeur of a mountain range or the infectious energy of a music festival – the ultra-wide lens ensures you get it all in.

Feeling creative? Explore the various shooting modes the GT 6T offers. Night mode is your secret weapon for capturing stunning photos even in low-light conditions. Say goodbye to grainy night-time memories – the GT 6T brightens up your nights! Portrait mode lets you achieve that sought-after bokeh effect, beautifully blurring the background to make your subject truly stand out. Perfect for capturing those Instagram-worthy portraits!

Don't forget about the power of video! The GT 6T allows you to record high-resolution videos, perfect for capturing those special moments in life. Whether it's your child's first steps or a hilarious moment with friends, the GT 6T preserves those memories in stunning detail. And with video stabilisation features, you can say goodbye to shaky footage – your videos will look smooth and professional.

Optimising Your Performance
The GT 6T is a powerful machine, but you can fine-tune it to perfectly match your usage patterns.

Access the Game Space feature, a one-stop hub for optimising your gaming experience. Free up resources, block notifications, and even customise performance settings to ensure your games run smoothly without any distractions.

For everyday tasks, explore the battery optimization settings. The GT 6T offers various power-saving modes to extend your battery life. Whether you need the phone to last the entire day or just want to squeeze out a few extra hours, there's a power-saving mode that perfectly fits your needs.

The Beauty Lies in the Details
The GT 6T is designed with the user in mind. The in-display fingerprint sensor unlocks your phone with a quick and secure touch. The phone also supports various gestures for added convenience, allowing you to perform specific actions with a swipe or a tap of the screen.

The Journey Begins
This chapter has been your introduction to the exciting world of the REALME GT 6T. We've explored its design, its features, and its potential. Now it's your turn to embark on your own journey of discovery. Explore the different features, personalise your phone, and unlock its full

potential. The GT 6T is more than just a phone; it's an extension of you, waiting to be explored. So, go forth, capture those moments, unleash your creativity, and experience the mobile world like never before!

Chapter 2: Setting Up Your REALME GT 6T

Congratulations on getting your hands on the realme GT 6T! Now, let's get you set up and ready to unleash its potential. This chapter will guide you through the initial steps, from inserting your SIM card to personalising your phone.

Inserting The SIM And SD Card

1. *Finding Your Tiny Gateway*: Flip your GT 6T over and locate the SIM tray on the bottom side. It might be a little inconspicuous, but you'll find a small indentation or hole beside it. This is where the SIM ejector tool (which came with your phone) comes into play.

2. *Pop it Out*: Gently insert the SIM ejector tool into the hole and press firmly. The SIM tray should eject slightly. Don't force it – a little pressure is all it takes.

3. *Time to Assemble*: Now, take a look at the SIM tray. You'll likely have two slots – one for your SIM card and another that might be designated for an SD card (if you're using one for extra storage). Carefully place your SIM card in the designated slot, making sure the gold contacts are facing downwards. If you're using an SD card, slide it into the appropriate slot as well.

4. *Homeward Bound*: Once everything is in place, carefully push the SIM tray back into the phone until it's secure and flush with the body. Easy peasy!

Powering On and Charging Up

1. *Juice Up*: Locate your charging cable (the one that came with your phone) and connect the USB Type-C end to the port on the bottom of your phone. Then, plug the other end into the power adapter. Finally, connect the power adapter to a wall outlet.

2. *Fueling for Adventure*: While your phone charges, it's a good idea to let it reach full capacity before your first use. This ensures it has the maximum juice to power you through those exciting setup steps.

3. *Waking Up Your GT 6T*: Once it's charged up, find the power button on the right side of the phone. Press and hold it for a few seconds until the realme logo lights up the screen. Voila! Your phone is springing to life.

Setting Up Your Language And Region

1. *Choosing Your Tongue*: After the initial boot-up, you'll be greeted by a language selection screen. Don't worry, you're not lost in translation! Simply scroll through the list and tap on the language you're comfortable with. This will be the language used for menus, settings, and displayed text on your phone.

2. *Location, Location, Location*: Next up, you'll be asked to choose your region. This helps set the correct date and time for your location and might also influence some phone features. Select the region that applies to you.

3. *Following the Guide*: Now comes the fun part – personalising your phone! You'll be guided through a series of prompts to complete the setup process. This might involve connecting to a Wi-Fi network, signing in to or creating a Google account (which gives you access to the Google Play Store and other

services), and setting up a screen lock to keep your data secure. Don't hesitate to take your time and read through the instructions – they're there to help you navigate this important step.

Chapter 3: Camera Quality and Features

The Realme GT 6T isn't just a phone; it's a powerful tool for capturing life's moments in stunning detail. This chapter dives deep into the world of the GT 6T's camera, helping you understand its settings, master the triple-camera system, and take photos that will wow your friends and family.

Understanding The Camera Settings And Modes

Imagine you're standing in front of a breathtaking landscape, wanting to capture its grandeur. Open the Camera app on your GT 6T – it's your window to those unforgettable moments. Here's a breakdown of some key features to navigate:

* *Finding Your Way Around*: Swiping right on the screen unveils a variety of shooting modes. Explore

Photo, Portrait, Video, and more – each designed to perfectly suit your creative vision.

* *Switching Cameras*: Want to capture a selfie with that stunning view? A simple tap on the little icon with two circles swaps between the powerful rear camera system and the high-quality front camera.

* *Zooming In for the Details*: Notice a captivating detail in the distance? The GT 6T lets you zoom in and out seamlessly. Pinch the screen or use the zoom toggle to get closer to the action, perfect for capturing wildlife or those candid moments with friends.

* *Lighting Up Your Shots*: Low-light conditions can be tricky, but fear not! The flash icon is your knight in shining armour. Choose "On" for a burst of light, "Auto" for the camera to decide, or "Off" if you're feeling creative with available lighting.

* *HDR*: Seeing the Bigger Picture: Imagine a photo that captures the vibrant colours of both a bright sky and the details in the shadows. That's the magic of HDR! Turn it "On" to allow the camera to take multiple exposures and blend them together for a photo that looks incredibly natural and detailed.

* *Depth Effect*: Making Your Subject Shine: Ever seen those portraits where the background is beautifully blurred, and the subject pops out in sharp focus? That's the Depth Effect in action! Activate it to achieve that professional-looking bokeh effect, perfect for highlighting your loved ones in photos.

* *Super Vivid Mode*: Colors That Pop: Feeling artistic? Super Vivid Mode is your secret weapon. It enhances the colour saturation in your photos, creating a striking and vibrant look that will make your photos stand out on social media.

* *Capture Timer*: You in the Picture Too!: Setting up a group photo or want to be part of the action yourself? The capture timer is your friend. Choose a 3-second or 10-second delay to give yourself time to strike a pose and jump in the frame.

* *Beauty Mode*: Looking Your Best: The built-in beauty filter can be your secret touch-up tool. With six levels to choose from, you can subtly enhance your skin tone, smooth out imperfections, and achieve a natural-looking glow.

Using The Triple Camera Setup

The GT 6T boasts a versatile triple-camera system on the back, ready to tackle any shooting scenario:

* *The Main Event*: The 50 MP Primary Camera: This powerhouse camera, equipped with a Sony LYT-600 sensor and optical image stabilisation (OIS), is your go-to for capturing stunning photos and videos in all lighting conditions. The large f/1.88 aperture allows more light to enter the sensor, resulting in sharp, detailed images even in low-light environments. OIS combats shakiness, ensuring crisp photos and smooth videos, even if you're not using a tripod.

* *Capturing the Big Picture*: The 8 MP Ultra-Wide Lens: Ever felt limited by the frame when trying to capture a breathtaking landscape or a group photo with everyone in it? The 8 MP ultra-wide lens comes to the rescue! This lens expands your field of view, allowing you to fit more into the frame, perfect for capturing expansive scenes, architectural marvels, or those fun group gatherings.

Tips for Taking Stunning Photos

Now that you're familiar with the camera app and the capabilities of the triple-camera system, let's unlock your inner photographer:

* *Unlocking Manual Controls*: Expert Mode for the Enthusiast: Feeling like you've mastered the basics and want to take more control over your shots? Expert Mode is your playground! Here you can adjust white balance, exposure, ISO, shutter speed, and more, giving you the freedom to fine-tune your photos for that professional look. Imagine you're photographing a vibrant sunset. Expert Mode allows you to adjust the white balance for warmer tones, perfectly capturing the fiery hues of the sky. Feeling adventurous with low-light photography? Play around with the ISO and shutter speed settings to achieve that artistic long exposure effect, transforming ordinary city lights into streaks of vibrant colour.

* *Capturing the Action*: Burst Mode: Let's say you're trying to capture that perfect action shot – your friend scoring the winning goal or your child's playful jump in the park. Burst mode is here to help! Hold down the shutter button, and the camera fires off a rapid sequence of photos, ensuring you capture that fleeting moment of

magic. Later, you can browse through the burst and pick the photo that perfectly freezes the action in time.

* *Finding the Perfect Angle*: Composition is Key Sometimes, a simple change in perspective can elevate your photo from good to great. Don't be afraid to move around your subject, crouch low, or even climb higher to find a unique angle. The GT 6T's large display lets you preview your shot perfectly, so you can experiment and see the results in real-time. Leading lines, the rule of thirds, and negative space are all basic composition techniques you can explore to add depth and interest to your photos.

* *Lighting is Everything*: Natural light is often your best friend. If possible, position yourself and your subject so that soft, diffused daylight falls on them. Harsh midday sun can create unwanted shadows, so consider shooting during the golden hours (sunrise or sunset) for the most flattering light. Indoors, look for bright windows or experiment with different lighting sources to create a mood or highlight your subject.

* *Editing Magic:* Making Your Photos Shine The GT 6T's built-in photo editor offers a variety of tools

to further enhance your photos. Adjust brightness, contrast, and saturation to fine-tune the look and feel of your image. Crop unwanted parts of the frame or straighten a tilted horizon. Play with filters to add a touch of artistic flair. Remember, editing is a powerful tool, but use it subtly to preserve the natural beauty of your photos.

By understanding your camera, using its features effectively, and experimenting with these creative techniques, you'll be well on your way to capturing stunning photos with your Realme GT 6T. So, grab your phone, get out there, and start creating visual memories that will last a lifetime!

Chapter 4: Advanced Camera Features

The Realme GT 6T's camera isn't just about capturing moments; it's about transforming them into artistic masterpieces. This chapter delves into some of the phone's most advanced features, helping you unlock creative potential and capture truly unforgettable photos.

Using Portrait Mode And Bokeh Effects

Imagine capturing a stunning portrait where your friend pops out in sharp focus, while the background melts into a dreamy blur. That's the magic of Portrait Mode! This feature allows you to achieve the coveted bokeh effect, a technique used by professional photographers to isolate and highlight the subject.

Here's how to unleash your inner portrait pro:

1. *fire up the camera app*: Grab your GT 6T and launch the Camera app. It's your gateway to creating stunning portraits.

2. *slide into portrait mode*: Swipe left on the screen until you see the "Portrait" icon. This activates the mode, transforming your camera into a tool for artistic expression.

3. *Focus on Your Subject*: Tap anywhere on the screen to focus on the person (or pet!) you want to be the star of the show. The GT 6T will ensure they are crisp and clear.

4. *Bluelicious Effects*: Look for a slider on the screen – this is your magic wand for controlling the background blur. Slide it to the right for a more intense blur, creating a dramatic effect that makes your subject truly stand out. For a more subtle touch, slide it to the left. Experiment and find the level of blur that perfectly complements your photo.

Night Mode And Low Light Photography

Low-light conditions can be a photographer's nemesis. But fear not, the GT 6T has a secret weapon: Night Mode. This innovative feature tackles darkness head-on, allowing you to capture stunning photos even in dimly lit environments.

Here's how to turn night into your artistic playground:

1. *Unleash the Night Owl*: Open the Camera app and swipe left until you see the "Night Mode" icon. Activate it, and let the GT 6T work its magic.

2. *Steady Does It*: Night Mode captures multiple photos with slightly different exposures. To ensure these images combine perfectly, it's important to hold your phone as steady as possible. Lean against a wall, or if you have one, use a tripod for ultimate stability.

3. *Light Up Your World*: Even in low light, the GT 6T might suggest using the flash for an extra boost. The choice is yours! Experiment with flash on and off to see which look you prefer.

Camera Flash and Timer: Your Essential Companions

While Portrait Mode and Night Mode push the boundaries of creativity, the GT 6T also offers essential features for everyday photography:

* *The Power of Flash*: The little lightning bolt icon on your screen is your flash control centre. Tap it to switch between "On" for a burst of light, "Auto" for the camera to decide based on lighting conditions, or "Off" if you're feeling creative and want to use available light.

* *The Timer*: You in the Picture Too! Planning a group photo or want to capture yourself amidst the scenery? The timer is your friend. Tap on the clock icon and choose a delay (3 seconds, 10 seconds) to give yourself time to strike a pose and jump into the frame.

By mastering these features and letting your creativity flow, you'll be well on your way to becoming a mobile photography whiz. So, grab your GT 6T, explore its capabilities, and transform everyday moments into extraordinary photos!

Chapter 5: Navigation and Gestures

Your Realme GT 6T is designed to be an extension of you, seamlessly integrating into your life. This chapter dives into the home screen, your launchpad to all things fun and functional, and unveils the magic of gestures – intuitive shortcuts that make navigating your phone a breeze.

Using The Home Screen And Navigation Bar

Imagine the home screen as your mission control centre. It's where you'll find everything you need to launch into action, from your favourite games and social media apps to essential tools and utilities. Dominating the screen is a grid of app icons, each representing a world of possibility waiting to be explored. The time widget keeps you on track, ensuring you never miss an important appointment or that live stream you've been eagerly waiting for.

Making the Home Screen Your Own

The beauty of the home screen lies in its customizability. Don't settle for a generic layout! Long press on any empty space to unleash a world of personalization options. Add your most-used apps for quick access, or banish rarely used ones to the app drawer (we'll get to that in a moment). Want to see your stunning vacation photos every time you pick up your phone? Turn a favourite picture into a wallpaper that reflects your style. The home screen is a canvas waiting for your creative touch.

The Navigation Bar: Your Friendly Guide

Think of the navigation bar as your constant companion at the bottom of the screen. It features three essential buttons to guide you through your digital journey:

* *Home Button*: A simple tap on this familiar icon brings you back to the home screen, no matter where you are in the phone's labyrinth of menus and apps. Getting lost? A quick press on the home button is your magic escape route.

* *Back Button*: Ever delve into an app or menu and suddenly realise you went a bit too deep? The back button is your knight in shining armour. A tap on

this button takes you back one step, allowing you to retrace your digital steps with ease.

* *Recent Apps Button*: Multitasking is a breeze with the Realme GT 6T. The recent apps button unveils a glimpse into your recently opened apps. Tap on an app preview to jump right back into it, or swipe it away to close it completely. This is a great way to switch between tasks or pick up right where you left off.

The Language of Gestures: Speaking to Your Phone

Gestures are like a secret handshake with your phone, allowing you to perform actions with a simple swipe or tap. Here are some cool gestures to add to your repertoire:

* *Swipe Up for Action*: Feeling the need to explore all the apps you've downloaded? A simple swipe up from the bottom of the screen banishes the home screen and ushers in the app drawer. Here, you'll find all your apps neatly organised, waiting to be launched.

* *Swiping Down for Knowledge*: Need a quick update on the latest news or want to adjust settings like Wi-Fi or Bluetooth? Simply swipe down from

the top of the screen to unveil the notification panel. This handy area houses your notifications and gives you quick access to frequently used settings. A further swipe down might reveal hidden brightness controls or allow you to activate features like aeroplane mode.

* *Double Tap to Wake Up*: Fumbling for the power button can be a thing of the past. The Realme GT 6T understands your impatience. A double tap on the screen when it's in sleep mode instantly brings it back to life, saving you precious seconds.

* *The Three-Finger Screenshot Masterclass*: Imagine capturing a funny meme or a friend's epic fail on social media. The three-finger screenshot is here to help! Simply swipe down on the screen with three fingers to capture an image of what's on your display. No more awkward button combinations or distorted screenshots – this is the smoothest way to snag what's on your screen.

These are just a few of the gestures that the Realme GT 6T has to offer. As you explore your phone, you'll discover even more ways to navigate with just a tap, swipe, or pinch. So, experiment, have fun, and unlock the full potential of your intuitive Realme GT 6T!

Chapter 6: Basic Phone Operations

Your Realme GT 6T it's a communication powerhouse. This chapter dives into the fundamental operations – making calls, sending texts, and managing contacts – ensuring you stay connected and informed with ease.

Making And Receiving Calls

Imagine you need to chat with a friend or have an important business call. The Phone app on your GT 6T is your gateway to making those connections. Here's a breakdown of making calls:

1. *Open the Phone App*: Look for the Phone icon on your home screen or app drawer. Tap on it to launch the app.

2. *Dialling In*: You'll see a keypad displayed on the screen. Use your finger to tap in the phone number you want to call. Don't worry if you make a mistake

– simply tap the backspace key (the one with the arrow) to erase a digit.

3. *Hitting Send*: Once you've entered the number, look for the big green phone icon at the bottom of the screen. This is your launch button! Tap on it, and your phone will initiate the call.

Answering the Call: Never Miss a Beat
Your phone rings, and it's your mom calling! To answer an incoming call, simply swipe up on the green phone icon that appears on your screen. This will connect you to the call, and you can start chatting.

Pro Tip: If you're expecting an important call but can't answer right away, you can also swipe up on the icon and then tap "Hold" to put the call on hold. This gives you a chance to silence any background noise or take a quick note before picking up.

Sending And Receiving Texts And MMS

Sometimes, a quick text is all you need. The Messages app on your GT 6T is your hub for sending and receiving text messages (SMS) and even multimedia messages (MMS) that can include pictures and videos. Here's how to send a text:

1. *Opening Messages*: Find the Messages icon on your app drawer and tap on it to launch the app.

2. *Starting a New Message*: Look for the "New message" icon, which is usually a plus sign (+) or a message bubble with a pencil. Tap on it to create a new message.

3. *Adding the Recipient*: You can add the recipient's phone number manually using the keypad or choose them from your contacts list. Simply tap on the "To" field and select the contact you want to message.

4. *Crafting Your Message*: Tap on the text field at the bottom of the screen and begin typing your message. Don't forget to use emojis to add some personality! Your GT 6T also offers features like voice typing and autocorrection to make texting even more convenient.

5. *Hitting Send*: Once you've crafted your perfect message, tap on the send icon (usually an arrow pointing upwards) to deliver your message.

Using The Phone Book And Contacts

Staying connected is easy when you have all your important contacts organised. The Contacts app on your GT 6T is your digital address book. Here's how to add a new contact:

1. *Opening Contacts*: Locate the Contacts icon on your app drawer and tap on it to open the app.

2. *Creating a New Contact*: Look for the "New Contact" button, which is often a plus sign (+) or a silhouette of a person. Tap on it to begin creating a new contact entry.

3. *Adding Details*: Your GT 6T allows you to store a variety of information for each contact, including their name, phone number, email address, and even a profile picture. Fill in the details you want to save for this contact.

4. *Saving It All*: Once you've entered all the information, tap on the "Save" button to add the new contact to your list.

Remember: Regularly updating your contacts ensures you always have the most recent information for your friends, family, and colleagues. This makes staying connected effortless!

By mastering these basic operations, you'll be well on your way to utilising your Realme GT 6T's communication features to the fullest.

Chapter 7: Understanding Settings

Your Realme GT 6T is a powerful tool, but like any good companion, it thrives on understanding your preferences. This chapter dives into the Settings app, your personal command centre for customising the phone to perfectly suit your style and needs.

Exploring The Settings App

Imagine your phone as a blank canvas. The Settings app is your paintbrush, brimming with colours and tools to create a user experience as unique as you are. Finding it is a breeze – simply swipe down from the top of your screen to access the notification panel. There, nestled amongst the icons, you'll find the gear icon – that's your gateway to the wonderful world of Settings.

Navigating the Settings Landscape

Opening the Settings app reveals a treasure trove of options, categorised into sections with clear and concise titles like "Display," "Sound," and "Privacy." Think of these sections as different rooms in a house – each one dedicated to a specific aspect of your phone's functionality. Within each section, you'll find a variety of settings you can adjust with a simple tap or toggle.

Feeling Lost? Search Comes to the Rescue!
Sometimes, even with clear categories, finding a specific setting can feel like searching for a needle in a haystack. But worry not, the search function is here to save the day! Located conveniently at the top of the Settings app, this is your secret weapon for navigating the vast landscape of options. Simply type in a keyword or phrase related to the setting you're looking for, and the app will instantly display relevant options, saving you precious time and frustration.

Customising Your Phone's Settings

Now that you know your way around, let's personalise your Realme GT 6T experience! Here are some key settings to explore and adjust:

* *Display Settings*: Setting the Stage for Visual Bliss: The display is your window to the digital world, so it makes sense to customise it to your preferences. Adjust the screen brightness to ensure comfortable viewing in any lighting condition. Feeling like a night owl? Enable Dark Mode for a more eye-pleasing experience during those late-night browsing sessions. And because a picture is worth a thousand words, personalise your wallpaper with an image that reflects your style or evokes a happy memory.

* *Sound Settings*: Finding Your Perfect Melody: Whether you're a music lover or a podcast enthusiast, customising the sound settings allows you to create the perfect soundscape. Adjust the ringtone and notification volumes to ensure you never miss an important call or message. Explore the equaliser options to fine-tune the audio output to your liking, whether you crave booming bass or crystal-clear highs.

* *Privacy Settings*: Your Data, Your Rules: In today's digital world, privacy is paramount. The Privacy Settings section empowers you to take control of your data. Manage app permissions to determine which apps have access to your location, camera, and other sensitive information. Feeling

location-conscious? Adjust your location settings to control when and how apps can access your location data.

* *Battery Settings*: Keeping Your Powerhouse Running Strong: The battery is the lifeblood of your phone. The Battery Settings section provides valuable insights into your battery usage patterns. Identify apps that are draining your battery and take steps to optimise their performance. When you need that extra boost to get through the day, enable power-saving modes to extend your battery life. For those who prioritise peak performance, the GT Mode is your secret weapon, unlocking the full potential of your phone's processing power.

Remember, this is just a glimpse into the vast array of customization options available in the Settings app. Feel free to explore different sections, experiment with settings, and discover features that make your Realme GT 6T truly your own.

Chapter 8: Screenshot and Screen Recording

Your Realme GT 6T isn't just a communication device; it's a window to your digital world. Sometimes, you'll stumble upon something hilarious, informative, or visually striking that you want to share or preserve for later. That's where screenshots and screen recordings come in – powerful tools that let you capture exactly what's on your screen with just a few clicks or swipes. Let's dive into how to master these features on your GT 6T.

How To Take Screenshots

Imagine you're browsing social media and come across a friend's outrageously funny meme. You want to share the laughter! Thankfully, capturing a screenshot on your GT 6T is a breeze. Here are three methods you can use:

* *The Classic Combo*: This is the most common method used across many smartphones. Hold down the power button, the one you use to turn your phone on and off, and the volume down button (the button closer to the bottom of the phone) – simultaneously! Hold them for a brief second, and you'll see a brief animation and hear a shutter sound (if enabled), indicating your screenshot is captured. A small preview will appear on the corner of your screen. Tap on the preview to edit or share it right away.

* *The Three-Finger Swipe*: Feeling fancy? This method is a bit more stylish. First, you need to enable the "3-Finger Screenshot" feature. Go to Settings > Convenience Tools > Gestures & Motions. Look for "3-Finger Screenshot" and make sure the toggle switch is turned on. Now, when you want to capture a screenshot, simply swipe down on your screen with three fingers – like you're giving the screen a little brush. Voila! Your screenshot is captured, and you'll see the familiar preview in the corner.

* *The Assistive Ball*: This method is perfect for those who want a little on-screen helper. Activate the "Assistive Ball" feature by going to Settings > Convenience Tools > Assistive Ball. Turn on the

48

toggle switch, and a small white circle will appear on the edge of your screen. You can customise what this button does, but for screenshots, we recommend choosing "Tap Menu". Now, whenever you want to capture a screenshot, simply tap the Assistive Ball, and a menu will pop up. Select "Screenshot" from the menu, and your screen will be captured.

How To Do Screen Recording

Let's say you're a gaming whiz and want to share your epic gameplay moves with the world, or maybe you're following a complex tutorial and want to record it for future reference. The screen recording feature on your GT 6T has you covered. Here's how to use it:

* *The Quick Panel Shortcut*: Swipe down from the top of your screen to access the Control Center, which is basically a treasure trove of handy shortcuts. Look for the "Screen recording" icon (it might look like a tiny camera recording a rectangle). Tap the icon, and a small red button will appear. Press the red button to start recording your screen. A timer will show you how long you've been recording, and a small red dot will appear at the top of your screen to indicate that recording is

in progress. When you're finished, simply tap the red dot or the notification bar to stop recording. Your screen recording will be saved to your phone's gallery, ready to be shared or reviewed later.

* *The Smart Sidebar Shortcut*: This method is for those who like to have their shortcuts readily available. Enable the Smart Sidebar by going to Settings > Smart Sidebar. From here, you can customise which features appear on the sidebar. Make sure to add "Screen Recording" to your sidebar. Now, when you want to record your screen, simply swipe the Smart Sidebar open from the right edge of your screen and tap the "Screen Recording" icon. Recording will start instantly, and you can stop it using the same method as the Control Panel shortcut.

Remember These Tips!
While capturing screenshots and screen recordings is a breeze, here are some helpful pointers to keep in mind:

- ❖ When recording the screen, other recording functions like voice messages or camera recording might be disabled.

- ❖ The recording will stop automatically if you turn off the screen, make a call, or power off the phone.
- ❖ Don't worry, you'll get a notification before the recording stops due to these actions.

So, there you have it! With these newfound screenshot and screen recording skills, you're well on your way to capturing and sharing those special digital moments on your smartphone.

Chapter 9: How to Download and Install Apps

Your Realme GT 6T is like a blank canvas, waiting for you to unleash its full potential. One of the most exciting ways to do that is by installing apps – those little pockets of creativity, productivity, and entertainment that make your smartphone experience truly personal. This chapter dives into the world of app installation on your GT 6T, guiding you through two main methods: venturing into the trusted Google Play Store and exploring installations from unknown sources.

Using The Google Play Store

Imagine a vibrant marketplace filled with endless possibilities. That's essentially what the Google Play Store is! It's the official app store for Android devices, boasting a massive collection of apps waiting to be discovered. Here's how to navigate this treasure trove:

1. *Unearthing the Play Store*: Look for the familiar Play Store icon on your home screen or app drawer. Tap on it, and voila! You're now in the app-quisition zone.

2. *The Search Bar*: Your App-finding Ally: Spot that magnifying glass icon at the top of the screen? That's your search bar – your gateway to a universe of apps. Type in the name of the app you have in mind, whether it's a game you've been wanting to try, a photo editing tool to unleash your inner artist, or a language learning app to broaden your horizons. Hit the search button, and let the exploration begin!

3. *Diving Deeper*: Exploring App Pages: From the search results, you'll see a list of apps that match your query. Tap on the one that piques your interest. This will take you to the app's dedicated page, brimming with information. See screenshots or even a short video preview to get a feel for the app's look and features. Read reviews from other users to get a sense of what others like (or dislike) about the app.

4. *The Glorious "Install" Button*: Feeling convinced this app belongs on your GT 6T? Look for the big, green "Install" button. Tap on it, and watch as the

app downloads and install itself onto your phone. The Play Store will keep you updated on the progress with a handy little bar.

5. *Welcome Aboard! Launching Your New App*: Once the installation is complete, you'll be presented with an "Open" button. Tap on it, and you're ready to dive into the app and explore its features! The app will also be neatly placed in your app drawer, ready to be launched whenever you need it.

Installing Apps From Unknown Sources

The Google Play Store offers a vast library of apps, but sometimes you might stumble upon an app that isn't available there. This is where installing apps from unknown sources, also known as sideloading, comes in. However, before we delve into this territory, it's crucial to understand the potential risks. Apps from untrusted sources could contain malware or viruses that can harm your device or steal your data. So, proceed with caution and only download apps from websites you know and trust.

Here's how to sideload an app, but remember, this is only recommended for advanced users who understand the risks involved:

1. *Unlocking the Gate*: Enabling Unknown Sources: Head over to your Settings menu. Navigate to the "Security" section. Look for the option that says "Unknown Sources" and toggle the switch on. This basically grants permission for your phone to install apps from outside the Google Play Store.

2. *Finding the Chosen One*: Downloading the APK File: Apps are typically downloaded in a format called APK (Android Package Kit). You'll need to download the APK file for the app you want to install. Ensure you download the file from a reputable and trusted website.

3. *Locating the Downloaded Treasure*: Once the download is complete, you might see a notification in your status bar. Swipe down to reveal the notification panel and tap on it. This will usually lead you to the downloaded file.

4. *Installation Time*: You might be prompted to confirm the app's permissions before proceeding. Review these permissions carefully to understand what data the app will access on your phone. If

you're comfortable, tap "Install" to begin the installation process.

5. *Welcome (if all goes well!):* Once the installation is complete, you should be able to find the app in your app drawer, ready to launch.

Remember, while sideloading opens doors to a wider variety of apps, it's important to prioritise safety. Always download apps from trusted sources and be cautious about the permissions

Chapter 10: Managing Your Apps

Ever felt like your phone's home screen resembles a cluttered toolbox? Fear not, Realme GT 6T user! This chapter equips you with the knowledge to transform your app haven from chaotic to cosmically organised.

How To Organise Your Apps

Imagine this: you reach for your phone, needing that fitness app to track your daily jog. But amidst a sea of icons, finding it feels like searching for a needle in a haystack. Let's conquer the clutter and organise your apps for effortless access:

* *The App Drawer*: A Hidden Gem: Your phone comes with an app drawer – a digital cabinet for all your apps. To activate it, navigate to Settings and enable "Drawer Mode". This keeps your home screen clutter-free while ensuring all your apps are just a swipe away.

* *Folding for Efficiency*: Creating Folders: Think of app folders as categorised mini-drawers within your app drawer. Group similar apps together – social media apps in one, games in another, and productivity tools in a third. To create a folder, simply hold down an app icon and drag it onto another related app. Poof! An instant folder appears, ready to be named and customised with icons.

* *Home Screen Zen*: Customising the App Layout: Don't underestimate the power of a well-organised home screen. Hold down an empty space to enter edit mode. Here, you can drag and drop app icons to create a layout that works for you. Place your most-used apps front and centre for quick access, and arrange others in a way that's visually pleasing and intuitive for you.

How To Uninstall And Update Apps

Just like your wardrobe, your phone's app collection needs occasional maintenance. Here's how to keep it clean and up-to-date:

* *Spring Cleaning Your Apps:* Uninstalling the Unwanted: Maybe you downloaded a game you

never play or an editing app you don't love. It's okay! Uninstalling unused apps frees up storage space and keeps your app drawer tidy. Head to Settings, then delve into "App management". Under "App list", find the app you want to say goodbye to. A long press on the icon usually initiates the uninstall process, though some system apps might require an extra tap into "App info" before revealing the uninstall button.

Staying on Top of Your Game: Updating Apps: New features, bug fixes, and security updates – these are the goodies that come with app updates. To ensure you have the latest and greatest, open the Google Play Store. Tap the menu icon, then select "My apps & games". Here, you'll see a list of apps with available updates. You can update them individually or tap the magic "Update All" button for a one-click refresh of all your apps. Remember, keeping apps updated is essential for optimal performance and security.

By following these tips, you'll transform your Realme GT 6T from an app sprawl into an organised oasis. So, categorise, declutter, and update – and take control of your digital world!

Chapter 11: How to Transfer Data from Your Old Phone

So, you've unwrapped your brand new Realme GT 6T, a sleek and powerful machine waiting to be unleashed. But before you dive headfirst into exploring its features, there's one crucial step: transferring your data from your old phone. Think of it like moving to a new house – you want to bring all your favourite things with you, from photos and music to contacts and messages. Here, we'll explore two methods to seamlessly bridge the gap between your old phone and your new GT 6T: using the built-in Clone Phone tool and transferring data through your computer.

Using The REALME GT 6T's Builtin Transfer Tool

The GT 6T comes with a built-in hero named Clone Phone, a champion of data migration. This nifty tool lets you transfer a whole bunch of stuff from your old phone to your new one, including:

- *Your Inner Circle*: Contacts, those all-important numbers that keep you connected to the world.
- *Message Magic*: Conversations, funny memes, and sentimental threads – all the digital whispers that tell your story.
- *App Oasis*: Your favourite apps, the ones you use for gaming, social media, or catching up on the news. No need to start from scratch!
- *Your Multimedia Stash*: Photos that capture memories, music that moves you, and documents that keep you organised.

Here's how to use Clone Phone and become a data transfer pro:

1. *Clone Phone on Both Phones*: It's like having a secret handshake! Install the Clone Phone app on both your old phone and your brand new GT 6T. You can usually find it pre-installed on the GT 6T, but if not, it's readily available for download from the app store.

2. *New Phone, Who Is?:* On your GT 6T, navigate to the Tools section (sometimes it might be hidden in Settings). Find Clone Phone and tap on it. A prompt will ask you to choose your role in this data

transfer drama. Since the GT 6T is your new home, select "This is the new phone."

3. *Your Old Phone – The Data Donor*: Grab your old phone and launch the Clone Phone app. Similar to the GT 6T, you'll be asked to choose your role. Since your old phone is generously donating its data treasures, select "This is the old phone."

4. *The QR Code Connection*: Your GT 6T will generate a unique QR code, like a digital passport for your data. Using the camera app on your old phone, scan this QR code. Voila! That's the magic handshake initiating the secure transfer process.

5. *Stay Close, Transfer Smoothly*: Imagine two dancers needing to be in sync. During the transfer, keep your phones close together. This ensures a stable Wi-Fi Direct connection, the invisible bridge that carries all your data to your new phone.

Transferring Data Using A Computer

Perhaps you're more comfortable using your computer as a data transfer hub. No worries, the GT 6T is happy to accommodate! Here's how to use your computer as a bridge:

1. *Cable Guy*: Grab your phone's data cable, the trusty cord that connects your phone to your computer's USB port. Plug one end into your old phone and the other into your computer.

2. *Charging Up:* Once connected, swipe down the notification bar on your old phone. You might see a notification indicating it's charging via USB. Look for an option that says "Tap for more options" or something similar. Select it, and then choose "Transfer files." This tells your computer that your phone is ready to exchange data.

3. *File Selection Frenzy:* Your computer should now recognize your old phone as an external storage device. Open a file explorer window and navigate to your old phone's storage. This is where the treasure hunt begins! Browse through folders like photos, music, documents, and downloads, selecting the files you want to transfer to your new GT 6T.

4. *The Great File Migration*: Once you've chosen your data warriors, copy them to a folder on your computer. Think of it as a temporary holding area. Once everything is copied, disconnect your old phone and connect your brand new GT 6T to the

computer using the data cable. Repeat steps 2 and 3 to establish a file transfer connection.

5. *New Phone, New Files*: Following the same logic, navigate to your desired folders on your GT 6T and paste the copied files from your computer. These could be photos that deserve a place on your new phone's stunning display, music that will fuel your next workout playlist, or important documents you need to keep close at hand.

Conquering The Transfer With Confidence
Whether you choose the convenience of Clone Phone or the familiarity of a computer-aided transfer, remember these helpful tips:

* *Battery Up:* Ensure both your old and new phones have a sufficient battery charge before starting the transfer process. The last thing you want is a data transfer interrupted by a dead battery!

* *Patience is a Virtue*: Transferring a large amount of data can take some time. Relax, grab a cup of coffee, or catch up on your favourite show while your data makes its way to your new phone.

* *Check Your Selection*: Before initiating the transfer, especially when using the computer method, double-check that you've selected the correct files you want to move to your GT 6T. No one wants to accidentally transfer old ringtones they no longer use!

Welcome to the GT 6T Family!
With your data successfully transferred, you're now officially a member of the GT 6T family! Your contacts are just a tap away, your favourite music is ready to pump up your jams, and your cherished memories are all neatly organised in your new phone's gallery. So, explore the features of your GT 6T, capture new moments with its powerful camera, and most importantly, enjoy the seamless user experience this phone offers. Welcome to a world of possibilities with the Realme GT 6T!

Chapter 12: How to Use the REALME GT 6T's Advanced Features

The Realme GT 6T isn't just a phone; it's an intelligent companion equipped with cutting-edge AI features that elevate your user experience. Imagine capturing stunning night shots, summarising lengthy articles in seconds, or cleaning up unwanted objects in photos with a simple tap. In this chapter, we'll delve into these remarkable AI features and explore how to personalise your phone's theme and wallpaper, making the GT 6T a true reflection of your unique style.

How To Use The Phone's AI Features

The GT 6T boasts a suite of AI features designed to make your life easier and more productive. Let's explore some of these gems:

* *AI Night Vision*: See the World in a New Light: Struggling to capture clear photos in dimly lit environments? Say goodbye to grainy pictures and hello to breathtaking low-light photography with AI Night Vision. This clever feature analyses the scene and intelligently adjusts settings to brighten shadows, reduce noise, and produce vibrant, detailed night shots. Now you can capture the magic of a starlit sky or the cosy ambiance of a candlelit dinner, all from the palm of your hand.

* *AI Smart Loop*: Become a Text Ninja: Ever stumbled upon a lengthy article you'd love to read, but short on time? AI Smart Loop comes to the rescue! This innovative feature uses artificial intelligence to analyse text and generate summaries. Simply highlight the portion you want summarised, and AI Smart Loop will condense it into a concise, easy-to-digest format. Perfect for catching up on news stories, research papers, or even long emails – all while maximising your time.

* *AI Smart Removal*: Edit Like a Pro: Let's face it, unwanted photobombers or distracting background elements can ruin a perfectly good picture. The GT 6T's AI Smart Removal feature puts the editing power in your hands. Select the object you want to eliminate, and I will cleverly remove it from your

photo, leaving you with a clean, polished image. This is especially handy for removing blemishes, stray power lines, or any other visual clutter that takes away from your photos.

* *AI Smart Search*: Knowledge at Your Fingertips: Imagine searching for anything on your screen, just by circling it! AI Smart Search makes it possible. Let's say you're reading an article about a fascinating historical landmark. Simply circle the name of the landmark on your screen, and AI Smart Search will instantly launch a web search, providing you with a wealth of information. This intuitive feature eliminates the need for multiple steps and lets you seamlessly explore topics that spark your curiosity.

How To Customise Your Phone's Theme And Wallpaper

The GT 6T understands that your phone is an extension of your personality. That's why it offers extensive customization options to transform its look and feel. Here's how to unleash your inner designer:

* *Theming Your Experience*: Head over to Settings > Wallpapers & style > Themes. Here, you'll discover a treasure trove of pre-designed themes, each offering a unique combination of wallpapers, icons, and fonts. Explore themes inspired by nature, vibrant cityscapes, or minimalist designs. With a simple tap, you can transform your phone's entire aesthetic to match your mood or preferences. Don't like the pre-designed options? No problem! The GT 6T allows you to download additional themes from the web, ensuring there's a perfect match for everyone.

* *A Touch of Personalization*: While themes offer a complete makeover, you can also personalise specific elements like wallpapers and icons. For a truly unique touch, set your favourite photo as the lock screen wallpaper. Imagine starting your day with a smile by seeing a picture of your loved ones or a cherished memory. You can even customise app icons to reflect your personality. Find an icon pack that matches your chosen theme or use a photo that represents a particular app (like a funny meme for your social media app).

By utilising the GT 6T's AI features and customization options, you're not just using a phone – you're crafting a digital experience that empowers you, entertains you, and reflects your unique style. So, explore, experiment, and have fun making the GT 6T your own!

Chapter 13: How to Set Up and Use Your Google Account

Congratulations on your new Realme GT 6T! It's a powerful tool waiting to be unleashed, and a big part of that power comes from connecting it to your Google Account. Think of it as your digital passport to a whole world of services and features. This chapter will guide you through the simple process of setting up and using your Google Account on your GT 6T, ensuring all your important information is seamlessly integrated.

New to the Googleverse? How To Create Your Account

Let's imagine you're venturing into a new land – Googleland, a vast and vibrant digital space. To become a citizen, you'll need a Google Account, your unique key that unlocks a treasure trove of benefits. Here's how to create one:

1. *Finding the Gateway*: On your GT 6T, locate the Settings app. It's usually represented by a cog or gear icon and acts as the control centre for your phone. Tap on it to open a treasure chest of customization options.

2. *The Path to Accounts*: Within Settings, scroll down a bit and find Accounts. This is the section where you'll manage all the different accounts you use on your phone, from social media to email. Tap on Accounts to open the door.

3. *Adding Your Google Identity*: At the bottom of the Accounts list, you'll usually see an option to Add Account. Consider it your official application to join Googleland! Tap on Add Account and a list of account types will appear.

4. *Choosing Your Guide*: Since we're on a Google Account quest, select Google from the list. This will initiate the account creation process, your trusty guide to becoming a Google citizen.

5. *Building Your Digital Home*: You'll be prompted to enter your first and last name. Fill in this information – it's what people will see when they interact with your Google Account online. Once you're happy, tap Next to continue the journey.

6. *Your Digital Address*: Now comes the fun part – creating your Gmail address! Think of it as your unique house number in Googleland. Gmail offers tons of storage for emails, so don't be afraid to get a little creative when choosing your address. Once you've picked your perfect Gmail name, tap Next to move forward.

7. *Building a Strong Gate*: Your password is like the gatekeeper to your digital home. Make sure it's strong and unique to prevent unwanted visitors. A good password is a combination of uppercase and lowercase letters, numbers, and symbols. Create your password, enter it again to confirm, and tap Next.

8. *Adding Security*: While not mandatory, adding your phone number to your account is a great way to recover it if you ever forget your password. Think of it as a backup key. If you choose to add your phone number, enter it here and tap Next.

9. *The Rules of the Land*: Before officially joining Googleland, it's important to understand the rules. Review the Terms of Service and Privacy Policy to ensure you're comfortable with how Google handles

your information. Once you've reviewed them, tap Accept to proceed.

10. *Welcome to the Googleverse!*: Follow any remaining prompts to finalise your account setup. Congratulations, you're now a Google Account holder!

How To Sync Your Data And Contacts

Now that you're a Google citizen, let's explore how to sync your data. Imagine you've met some amazing people in Googleland and you want to stay connected. Syncing allows you to seamlessly share information between your GT 6T and your Google Account, ensuring you always have your important data with you. Here's how to set up syncing:

1. *Revisiting the Settings Gateway*: Just like before, head back to the Settings app on your GT 6T. Remember, it's the control centre for your phone's functionality.

2. *The Path to Accounts*: Navigate to the Accounts section once again. This is where you'll manage all the different accounts you use on your phone.

3. *Finding Your Google Home*: Look for the Google account you just created and tap on it. This will open a new menu with various options related to your account.

4. *Unlocking the Sync Vault*: Look for a setting labelled Account sync or something similar. This is the treasure chest where you control what data gets synced between your phone and your Google Account. Tap on Account sync to open it.

5. *Choosing What to Share*: Here's where the magic happens! You'll see a list of different data categories like Contacts, Calendar, Docs, and Photos. Each category has a toggle switch. To sync a specific type of data, simply turn on the toggle switch next to it. For instance, to ensure your contacts are always up-to-date across your devices, make sure the Contacts toggle is switched on.

6. *Taking Manual Control*: If you ever need to update your data immediately, you can force a sync. Tap the three dots in the top right corner and select Sync now. This will manually push any changes you've made on your phone to your Google Account, and vice versa.

Congratulations! You've successfully set up your Google Account and enabled syncing on your Realme GT 6T. Now, your contacts, calendar events, and other important data will be seamlessly integrated between your phone and your Google Account. This ensures you can access your information from any device, keeping you connected and organised no matter where you go!

Remember:
- ❖ A Google Account unlocks a vast ecosystem of Google services, from Gmail and Google Drive to YouTube and the Play Store. Explore these apps to experience the full potential of your Google Account.
- ❖ Keeping your Google Account information secure is important. Use a strong password and enable two-factor authentication for added security.

With your Google Account up and running, you're well on your way to conquering the digital world with your Realme GT 6T!

Chapter 14: How to Use the Camera And Take Stunning Videos

Your Realme GT 6T isn't just a phone; it's a pocket-sized powerhouse waiting to capture your world in stunning motion. This chapter dives deep into the world of video on your GT 6T, transforming you from a casual snapper to a video maestro. Get ready to explore the different video modes, harness the power of the triple-camera system, and capture unforgettable moments with crystal-clear quality.

Understanding Video Modes And Settings

Every great filmmaker needs the right tools, and the GT 6T offers a treasure trove of video options to fit any creative vision. Here's a breakdown of some key features that will have you shooting like a pro:

* *Resolution Revolution*: Imagine the difference between a grainy, pixelated home movie and a cinema-quality blockbuster. That's the power of resolution! Choose between 720p, 1080p, and even stunning 4K resolution[2]. Higher resolutions result in sharper, more detailed videos, perfect for capturing those epic landscapes or life's precious moments in all their glory.

* *Frame Rate Frenzy*: Frame rate refers to the number of images (frames) captured per second. Think of it like a flipbook – the more frames you have, the smoother the motion. The GT 6T offers 30fps and 60fps recording options[2]. For everyday videos, 30fps is a great choice. But if you're aiming for that super smooth, slow-motion effect (think action movies!), bump it up to 60fps and capture every detail of that winning jump shot or your pet's playful antics.

* *Steady Does It:* Shaky videos can be a recipe for nausea. The GT 6T comes equipped with both Electronic Image Stabilization (EIS) and Optical Image Stabilisation (OIS)[2] – your secret weapons against shaky footage. EIS uses software to compensate for minor hand movements, while OIS utilises a physical mechanism to stabilise the camera lens itself. The result? Crystal-clear,

smooth videos that will have you looking like a seasoned videographer.

* *Slow Motion Magic*: The world around us moves fast, but with the GT 6T, you can slow it all down and savour the details. The slow-motion mode lets you capture fleeting moments at 1080p resolution and 120fps, or even a mind-bending 720p at 240fps[2]. Imagine the dramatic effect you can create as your friend dives into the pool or your dog chases a butterfly – all stretched out in slow-motion glory!

* *Time-lapse Mastery*: Ever wondered how those cool videos are made where clouds seem to race across the sky or traffic flows by in a blur? That's the power of time-lapse! This mode condenses long periods into shorter clips, perfect for showcasing sunrises, bustling cityscapes, or the construction of a Lego masterpiece.

* *Dual Power, Double the Fun*: Unleash the power of multiple perspectives with the Multi-view Recording feature[2]. Imagine capturing yourself giving a presentation while simultaneously recording the reactions of the audience from a different angle. This innovative feature opens doors for creative storytelling and engaging video content.

How To Use The Triple Camera Setup

The GT 6T boasts a triple-camera system, a versatile trio ready to tackle any filming situation. Let's meet the stars of the show:

* *The Main Man*: The 50 MP Primary Camera: This is your go-to camera for most situations. With a whopping 50 megapixels, it captures stunning detail and clarity, ensuring your videos are crisp and vibrant[1]. Phase Detection Auto Focus (PDAF) keeps your subject sharp, while Optical Image Stabilization (OIS) says goodbye to shaky footage.

* *The Scene Stealer*: The 8MP Ultra-Wide Camera: Ever feel like you can't quite squeeze everything into the frame? The 8MP ultra-wide camera comes to the rescue with its expansive 112° field of view[1]. This is your best friend for capturing breathtaking landscapes, grand architecture, or those unforgettable group photos that always seem to leave someone out. Now, you can fit everyone (and everything) in with ease!

Lights, Camera, Action! Capturing Epic Videos and Group Fun

Filming with your GT 6T is as simple as unlocking your creative potential. Open the camera app, switch to video mode (usually indicated by a video camera icon), and tap the record button to start capturing your masterpiece. For group videos, the ultra-wide camera is your best bet – you can fit the entire crew in the frame, ensuring no one gets left out of the fun.

Pro Tips for Shooting Like a Star
Now that you've unlocked the treasure trove of video features on your GT 6T, here are some pro tips to elevate your videography game:

* *Be a Lighting Ninja*: Lighting is key to any great video. Natural light is your best friend, so whenever possible, shoot outdoors or find a well-lit environment indoors. If you must film in low light, try to find additional sources of illumination.

* *Steady Wins the Race*: Shaky footage can be a real mood-killer. Hold your phone firmly with both hands and engage the OIS feature for maximum stability. If you can, consider using a tripod for even smoother videos, especially for long shots or time-lapses.

* *Mind the Focus*: Ensure your subject is always in sharp focus. Tap the screen to focus on a specific area while recording. The GT 6T's PDAF will help you achieve clear and crisp videos.

* *Get Creative with Angles*: Don't be afraid to experiment with different camera angles! Try shooting from a low angle for a dramatic effect, or get high up for a stunning birds-eye view. Explore different perspectives to add visual interest to your videos.

* *Embrace the Edit*: Once you've captured your footage, don't be afraid to edit it! The GT 6T has a built-in video editor, or you can download a third-party app to add music, titles, and transitions. Editing can take your videos from good to great!

So, are you ready to become a video whiz? Grab your Realme GT 6T, unleash your creativity, and start capturing life's moments in stunning cinematic quality. With the powerful camera system, versatile video modes, and these helpful tips, you'll be a master filmmaker in no time!

Chapter 15: How to Customise Your Home Screen and Notifications

Imagine your Realme GT 6T not just as a phone, but as an extension of yourself. A digital canvas waiting to be personalised to reflect your unique style and preferences. This chapter dives into the world of customization, guiding you through transforming your home screen and notification shade into spaces that work for you.

How To Add And Remove Widgets

The home screen is your phone's prime real estate, and widgets are like handy tools you can place on it. Think of them as mini-apps that give you quick access to information or features you use all the time. Here's how to make widgets your customization companions:

* **Adding Widgets**:

1. *Long press the party*: Give an empty spot on your home screen a long press, like a firm handshake initiating the customization process. Alternatively, you can pinch the screen with two fingers to initiate the same effect.

2. *The Widget Wonderland*: A menu will appear, and you'll see an option for "Widgets." Tap on it, and a treasure trove of widgets will unfold before your eyes. Explore the options – weather updates, music controls, a quick calendar glimpse – there's a widget for almost everything!

3. *Finding Your Perfect Fit*: Once you've found a widget that sparks joy (or usefulness!), tap and hold it to enter selection mode. Drag it to your desired location on the home screen. Think about the apps you use most – a music widget close to where you launch your favourite tunes, or a calendar widget near your clock for a quick glance at your schedule.

4. *Sealing the Deal*: Once you've positioned your widget perfectly, simply lift your finger, and voila! Your new home screen buddy is ready to serve you.

* **Saying Goodbye to Widgets**:

We all evolve, and so can your home screen! If a widget is no longer bringing you joy, here's how to send it packing:

1. *A Long Farewell*: Long press the widget you want to banish to the digital abyss.

2. *The Goodbye Swipe*: While holding the widget, gently swipe it towards the "Remove" or "Trash" icon that appears at the top or bottom of your screen, depending on your phone's model. Think of it as a digital wave goodbye.

3. *Letting Go*: Release your finger, and the widget will disappear from your home screen, making space for new customizations.

How To Customise Your Notification Shade

The notification shade is like a message centre, a hub for all the alerts and updates from your apps. But let's be honest, sometimes it can feel like information overload. Here's how to customise your notification shade to ensure it informs you without overwhelming you:

* **Taming the App Noise**:

1. *Settings Sanctuary*: Let's head to the "Settings" app. It's usually represented by a cog or gear icon and acts as the control centre for your phone. Tap on it to enter the customization zone.

2. *Finding Your Notification Voice*: Look for a section labelled "Notifications & status bar" or something similar. This is where you'll find the

tools to fine-tune how your phone notifies you. Tap on it to explore the options.

3. *App-by-App Approach*: You'll see a list of all your apps. Think of them as students in a classroom, and you get to decide the notification rules for each. Tap on the individual app you want to adjust.

4. *Striking the Balance*: Here, you'll see options to enable or disable notifications for that specific app. Maybe you want to silence game notifications entirely, while keeping email alerts active. The choice is yours! Use the toggle switch next to each option to make your selections.

* **Lighting Up Your Life (or Not):**
1. *Settings Sanctuary (Again!):* Sometimes, a silent notification might be missed. If you prefer a visual cue, you can enable a notification light. Head back to "Settings" if you're not already there.

2. *Illuminating Options*: Navigate to the "Display and brightness" section. This is where you control the visual aspects of your phone's screen. Tap on it to delve deeper.

3. *Edge Light Up:* Look for an option called "Screen Light Effect" or something similar. Here, you can customise the way the edges of your phone's screen light up for notifications. Maybe you prefer a subtle glow, or a vibrant pulse to grab

your attention. Play around with the settings to find what suits your style.

Remember, customization is a journey, not a destination! Don't be afraid to experiment with widgets, notification settings, and even themes (available for download in most app stores) to create a home screen and notification shade that reflects your personality and keeps you informed efficiently. The Realme GT 6T is your canvas, and you are the artist!

Bonus Tip: Explore the Power of Gestures
Want to take your customization a step further? The Realme GT 6T supports a variety of gestures that allow you to interact with your phone in a more intuitive way. For instance, you can perform a double tap to wake the screen or draw a specific letter on the display to launch a quick app. Head over to "Settings" and explore the "Gestures" section to discover the options and personalise your phone experience even more.

Chapter 16: How to Troubleshoot Common Issues

Let's face it, even the most amazing tech can encounter occasional hiccups. But fear not, GT 6T warrior! This chapter equips you with the knowledge to troubleshoot common issues and keep your phone running smoothly.

How To Fix Common Problems And Errors

Battery Blues: Battling Against Drain
Noticing your battery disappearing faster than a magician's rabbit? Here are some detective skills to help you identify the culprit:

* *Screen Sleuth*: The culprit might be right under your nose (or should we say, fingers). Head to your Settings and navigate to the Battery section. Here, you'll find a nifty feature called "Show full device usage." This unveils which apps are hogging the most battery life. Games and video streaming

services are common culprits, so if you see an app dominating the chart, consider limiting your playtime or finding a more battery-friendly alternative.

* *Brightness Battle*: A super bright screen is beautiful, but it can also be a battery drain. Dimming your screen a notch or enabling auto-brightness can significantly improve battery life.

* *Notification Ninjas*: Those persistent notification pop-ups might seem harmless, but they can drain your battery in the background. Dive into your app settings and disable notifications for apps that you don't need constant updates from. Trust us, your battery will thank you!

* *Location, Location, Location Services*: GPS, Wi-Fi, Bluetooth – these connectivity features are fantastic, but they can be battery guzzlers. Make sure to turn them off when you're not actively using them. Think of it as giving your phone a chance to breathe.

* *The Doze Option*: Did you know your phone can take a power nap? Enable the "Screen Timeout" option in your settings to turn off the screen after a

set period of inactivity. The fewer those pixels are lit up, the more juice your battery retains.

* *Update Yourself*: Software updates often come with bug fixes and performance improvements, which can sometimes translate to better battery life. So, keep your GT 6T updated with the latest software to ensure optimal performance.

* *Charging Champions*: While it's tempting to keep your phone plugged in all night, constantly topping up the battery can negatively impact its lifespan. Try to unplug your phone when it reaches around 100% charge.

Screen Shenanigans: When Your Display Misbehaves
A frozen or unresponsive screen can be a real buzzkill. But don't panic! A simple force restart can often work wonders. Press and hold the power button for a few seconds (usually around 10-15 seconds) until the phone restarts. This can clear minor glitches and get your display back on track.

Freezing Frustrations: When Your Phone Gets Stuck
If your phone is experiencing freezing episodes, it might be an app causing the trouble. Think about

any recent app installations that coincided with the freezing issue. Try uninstalling those apps one by one to see if the problem persists. By process of elimination, you can identify the app culprit and banish it from your phone.

Network No-Shows: Conquering Connectivity Issues

Having trouble connecting to Wi-Fi or mobile data? Don't fret! Here's a troubleshooting toolkit:

* *The Power Cycle*: Sometimes, a simple restart of both your phone and your router can work wonders. Turn them both off for a few seconds, then power them back on and see if the connection is restored.

* *Update Army:* Outdated software can sometimes lead to connectivity issues. Ensure your phone has the latest software updates installed.

How To Use The Builtin Troubleshooting Tools

Your Realme GT 6T comes with some handy built-in tools to help you diagnose and fix problems:

* *Recovery Mode*: Think of this as your phone's emergency room. In case of major software issues, you can access Recovery Mode to perform a factory reset, clear the cache partition, or update the software using an SD card. (Remember, a factory reset wipes all your data, so proceed with caution and always back up your data beforehand!)

* *Safe Mode*: Suspect a third-party app is causing trouble? Safe Mode is your knight in shining armour. Booting your phone in Safe Mode temporarily disables all third-party apps, allowing you to see if the issue persists. If everything works smoothly in Safe Mode, then a downloaded app is likely the culprit. You can then uninstall apps one by one to identify the problematic one.

* *Factory Reset*: As a last resort, if you're facing persistent issues that defy other solutions, a factory reset can be your nuclear option. This wipes your phone clean, restoring it to its original factory settings. While it can be effective, it also erases all your data, photos, contacts, and downloaded apps. So, always, always, always back up your data before performing a factory reset.

Remember, you are not alone! The internet is a vast resource for troubleshooting information. Search online forums or the Realme website for specific error messages or issues you encounter. The GT 6T user community is vast and helpful, and you're sure to find solutions and tips from other users.

The Final Word: Prevention is Key
Many of these troubleshooting tips can be applied as preventative measures. Regularly updating your software, keeping your apps organised, and monitoring battery usage can help prevent problems from arising in the first place. By following these simple steps, you can ensure your Realme GT 6T continues to be your loyal tech companion for years to come.

Chapter 17: How to Update and Back Up Your Phone

Keeping your Realme GT 6T in tip-top shape is about more than just a cool phone case (although, we won't judge your love for a flashy cover!). Regular software updates and data backups are the unsung heroes of phone maintenance, ensuring your device runs smoothly, securely, and holds onto your precious memories.

How To Update Your Phone's Software

Imagine your phone as a superhero. Software updates are like giving it a cool new gadget or a power-up. These updates often include bug fixes, security patches, and even new features that make your phone even more awesome. Here's how to keep your GT 6T updated and ready to tackle any digital challenge:

* *Calling on the Official Reinforcements*: First things first, head over to the official Realme

website. Think of it as the headquarters for all things Realme. There, you'll find the latest software update tool – your phone's very own superhero sidekick. Download this tool, and get ready to unleash its power!

* *Gearing Up for the Update*: Plug your GT 6T into your computer using its trusty USB cable. This creates a secure connection to transfer the update.

* *Introducing the Update Assistant*: The downloaded tool will most likely prompt you to install an "Update Assistant" on your phone. Consider it a mini-program that will guide you through the update process. Follow the on-screen instructions, and soon, this assistant will be working its magic.

* *Scouting the Update Landscape*: Once the Update Assistant is up and running, it will show you two important things: the current software version on your phone and any available updates. Think of it as an update roadmap!

* *Supercharge Your Phone (Literally!):* Before hitting the download button, make sure your phone has at least 50% battery power. Updates can take a while, and you don't want your phone running out

of juice in the middle of the process. Plus, a fully charged phone ensures a smoother update experience.

Download and Install: With everything in place, tap that download button and let the update magic begin! The Update Assistant will download the latest software version and install it on your phone. This might take a few minutes, so sit back, relax, and maybe catch up on some videos (on another device, of course!).

How To Back Up Your Data And Contacts

Our phones hold a treasure trove of memories – photos, messages, contacts – and the thought of losing them can be a nightmare. Backups are your digital safety net, ensuring this information is protected even if your phone encounters a glitch. Here's how to create backups using two methods: locally on your phone and using Google Drive:

Method 1: The Local Backup Battalion

* *Mission Control*: Access your phone's settings. Think of it as the command centre for all things

phone-related. Navigate to "Backup and reset" – this is where you'll find your backup tools.

* *Choosing Your Backup Squad*: Within the backup settings, you'll see a selection of data you can back up. This can include your contacts, messages, call logs, even your phone's settings and preferences. It's like creating a digital army of your important information. Choose the data you want to safeguard.

* *Initiating the Backup*: Once you've selected your data, tap the "Start" button. This will be like giving the backup process the green light. The backup file will be stored on your phone's internal storage, so make sure you have enough space available.

* *Double Duty – Backup to Computer*: Backing up locally is great, but for extra security, consider copying the backup file to your computer. Connect your phone to your computer and use a file transfer program to locate and save the backup file. Think of it as having a secret code stored in two locations, just in case!

Method 2: The Google Drive Cavalry

* *Summoning the Google One App*: For a cloud-based backup solution, the Google One app is your knight in shining armour. If you haven't already, download the app and sign in with your Google account.

* *Reporting for Duty*: Open the Google One app and tap on "Storage." This will show you an overview of your storage usage across various Google services, including your phone's backup.

* *Activating Backup*: If this is your first phone backup using Google Drive, tap on "Set up data backup" followed by "Backup now." If you've backed up before, you'll see an option to "View details" or "Backup now," depending on your preference. Choose "Backup now" to initiate a fresh backup.

* *Managing Your Backup*: To see what data is currently backed up to your Google Drive and manage your backup settings, tap on "Manage backup" within the Google One app. Here, you can choose to back up specific data types or schedule automatic backups.

Remember, updating your phone and backing up your data are like putting on your phone's superhero cape. These practices ensure your GT 6T stays protected, secure, and ever-ready to tackle any digital challenge!

Bonus Tip: Embrace Automation!
Many phones, including the Realme GT 6T, offer the option to enable automatic software updates. This ensures you always have the latest security patches and features without having to remember to download them manually. Consider enabling this option in your settings for a truly set-it-and-forget-it approach to keeping your phone up-to-date.

Conclusion

Welcome to the summary of this exciting world of the Realme GT 6T! This guide is your launchpad to mastering your new tech companion. Get ready to dive into the phone's features and summary of the whole story or will I say, some key take away.

Summary Of Key Takeaways

Tech Specs That Impress
The GT 6T isn't just a phone – it's a powerhouse. Imagine a super-speedy Snapdragon 7+ Gen 3 chipset – that's the brain powering everything you do on your phone, from lightning-fast browsing to running demanding games. And let's not forget the stunning 6.78-inch AMOLED display. Think vibrant colours, deep blacks, and a super smooth 120Hz refresh rate – scrolling will feel like butter on toast (or perhaps a more appropriate analogy – silk on a racing car's hood?).

Built to Last, Built to Play

Powering through your day? No problem. The GT 6T boasts a massive 5500mAh battery, like a reliable friend with a never-ending supply of juice. And when it's time to recharge, the 120W fast charging technology is your superhero. Imagine going from near dead to battle-ready in just a few minutes – that's the kind of power you deserve.

Capture Every Moment

Memories are precious, and the GT 6T helps you capture them in stunning detail. The dual 50 MP main camera is your window to the world, letting you take sharp, crystal-clear photos. And for those breathtaking landscapes or capturing the whole gang in a selfie, the 8MP ultrawide camera has you covered. Plus, with a 32 MP front camera, your selfies will be on point, ready to dominate your social media feed.

Your Phone, Your Way

The GT 6T isn't just powerful, it's personal. Realme UI 5.0 puts you in control, with a user-friendly interface and tons of customization options. Want a wallpaper that reflects your style? Done. Wish to organise your apps in a way that makes sense to you? Easy! This phone is an extension of you, and Realme UI 5.0 empowers you to make it your own.

Tips For Getting The Most Out Of Your REALME GT 6T

Now that you've got the GT 6T basics down, here are some pro tips to take your phone experience to the next level:

* *Battery Boss*: Become a battery life master! Reduce screen brightness when you don't need it maxed out, and close any apps you're not actively using. Think of it as giving your phone a chance to breathe and conserve its energy. Also, turn off Wi-Fi and Bluetooth when you're not connected to save some extra juice.

* *Camera Chameleon*: Unleash your inner photographer! The GT 6T's camera is versatile, so experiment with the different modes. Try portrait mode for stunning bokeh effects, or explore the night mode to capture clear photos even in low-light conditions. There's a whole world of creative possibilities waiting to be explored.

* *Storage Savvy*: Keep your phone's storage happy! Get in the habit of regularly deleting unnecessary files, like old photos or videos you don't need anymore. Also, uninstall apps you don't use –

think of it as giving your phone a digital decluttering session.

* *Protected Warrior*: Accidents happen, so safeguard your GT 6T! Invest in a screen protector and a case. They'll be your phone's knights in shining armour, guarding it against scratches, bumps, and the occasional drop.

* *Update Updater*: Stay on top of your game! Enable automatic software updates to ensure your phone has the latest security patches and features. Think of it as keeping your phone's software suit up-to-date and ready to tackle any digital challenge.

The Realme GT 6T is more than just a phone; it's a powerful companion for your digital adventures. With this guide and a little exploration, you'll be a GT 6T master in no time!

www.ingramcontent.com/pod-product-compliance
Lightning Source LLC
Chambersburg PA
CBHW050116230526
45470CB00004B/1852